Think Tiny, Grow Big

Think Tiny, Grow Big

Matthew Petchinsky

Think Tiny, Grow Big: The Minimalist Mindset
By: Matthew Petchinsky

Introduction: The Minimalist Mindset as a Path to Transformation

In a world that often glorifies excess, speed, and accumulation, the concept of minimalism offers a profound counterbalance—a transformative mindset that focuses not on having more, but on valuing less. Minimalism isn't just about decluttering your living space or downsizing your possessions; it's about creating intentionality in every aspect of your life. It's a shift in perspective that allows you to focus on what truly matters, cutting through the noise of an overstimulated and overwhelming world.

At its core, minimalism is not a rejection of possessions or ambition; rather, it's a commitment to clarity and purpose. By choosing to eliminate what doesn't serve your goals, values, or happiness, you create space—physically, mentally, and emotionally—for what truly does. This transformation begins with understanding that minimalism is not a one-size-fits-all approach. Instead, it's a deeply personal journey of aligning your life with your unique priorities.

The Benefits of Minimalism in a Fast-Paced World

In today's society, where we're constantly bombarded with information, advertisements, and the pressure to achieve more, it's easy to feel lost in the chaos. The pursuit of "more" often leads to stress, burnout, and a sense of emptiness. Minimalism offers an antidote to this frenetic pace by encouraging us to slow down, assess, and simplify.

Minimalism can:

1. Reduce Stress: Letting go of physical and mental clutter brings a sense of relief and calm. With fewer distractions, you can focus on what truly matters, reducing decision fatigue and anxiety.
2. Enhance Productivity: By streamlining your environment and commitments, minimalism helps you prioritize tasks and goals, improving efficiency and effectiveness.
3. Improve Well-being: Simplifying your life allows you to make room for joy, connection, and experiences that bring true fulfillment, rather than fleeting satisfaction.
4. Cultivate Financial Freedom: Minimalism encourages mindful spending, helping you break free from the cycle of consumerism and redirect your resources toward meaningful investments.
5. Foster Clarity and Intentionality: With a minimalist mindset, you learn to distinguish between what adds value to your life and what detracts from it, creating a life aligned with your core values.

The Path to Exponential Growth

The minimalist mindset isn't just about decluttering your home or reducing possessions—it's a foundation for exponential growth in all areas of life. By eliminating distractions, you unlock the power of focus and intentionality, enabling you to pursue your goals with greater clarity and determination.

- Clarity: A cluttered environment often reflects a cluttered mind. When you embrace minimalism, you clear both your space and your thoughts, allowing you to see your goals and priorities more vividly.
- Productivity: Simplifying your commitments and focusing on fewer, more meaningful tasks allows you to achieve more in less time. The energy saved from decision fatigue and mental clutter can be redirected toward creativity and innovation.
- Personal Fulfillment: Minimalism helps you break free from the cycle of chasing external validation and fleeting pleasures. Instead, you focus on experiences, relationships, and achievements that bring long-term satisfaction and a deeper sense of purpose.

A Roadmap to Change

This book will guide you through the principles and practices of the minimalist mindset, offering practical strategies to integrate this philosophy into your daily life. Whether you're looking to declutter your physical space, simplify your schedule, or gain clarity on your life's purpose, this book provides actionable insights to help you transform your life.

Minimalism isn't about deprivation—it's about liberation. It's about reclaiming your time, energy, and focus, so you can channel them into what truly matters. By adopting the minimalist mindset, you'll discover that less truly can be more—not just in possessions, but in clarity, productivity, and personal fulfillment.

Are you ready to embrace the power of simplicity and embark on a journey toward exponential growth? Let's begin.

Chapter 1: Defining Minimalism for the Mindset Shift

Minimalism is a term that often conjures images of bare walls, sparse furniture, and a life devoid of luxuries. While these aesthetic interpretations might reflect certain aspects of minimalism, they fail to capture its essence as a transformative mindset. Minimalism, at its core, is not about depriving yourself or living in extremes—it is about prioritizing what adds value to your life and letting go of what does not.

In this chapter, we'll dive deep into the true meaning of minimalism, dispel some common myths, and explore the profound psychological benefits it offers. By shifting your perspective, you'll begin to see how a minimalist mindset can clear the path for personal growth, new opportunities, and a more fulfilling life.

What Minimalism Truly Means

At its heart, minimalism is the art of intentional living. It's about identifying the things, relationships, and commitments that bring you joy, align with your values, or help you grow—and consciously letting go of everything else. It is not a rigid lifestyle or a prescriptive rulebook but a flexible and personal approach to creating a life that feels meaningful and manageable.

Minimalism is about:

1. **Clarity over Clutter:** Simplifying your life so you can focus on what matters most.
2. **Quality over Quantity:** Prioritizing meaningful experiences and relationships over material possessions.
3. **Purposeful Living:** Aligning your choices with your long-term goals and values.

However, before diving deeper, it's essential to address some misconceptions that can hinder people from embracing this mindset.

Debunking Common Myths About Minimalism

1. **"Minimalism Means Owning Nothing"** Minimalism is not about living with as little as possible. It's about living with *what matters.* If you love books, a minimalist life might include a carefully curated library. If travel is your passion, minimalism might mean simplifying your home life to afford more adventures.

2. **"Minimalism is Only for the Privileged"** While social media often portrays minimalism as sleek interiors and expensive simplicity, the essence of minimalism is accessible to everyone. It's about making intentional choices, regardless of your financial situation or lifestyle.

3. **"Minimalism is Cold and Emotionless"** On the contrary, minimalism often fosters deeper emotional connections. By removing distractions and excess, you make room for meaningful relationships, purposeful work, and fulfilling experiences.

4. **"Minimalism Requires Extreme Sacrifice"** Minimalism is not about denying yourself pleasure or comfort. Instead, it encourages mindful consumption and intentional living, allowing you to savor and appreciate the things you choose to keep.

The Psychological Benefits of Letting Go

One of the most transformative aspects of minimalism is its impact on your mental well-being. By decluttering your environment and your mind, you create space for calm, clarity, and intentionality. Here are some of the key psychological benefits of letting go:

1. **Reduced Stress** Physical and mental clutter can feel overwhelming. When your space is chaotic, it's difficult to feel relaxed or in control. Letting go of unnecessary possessions, commitments, or thoughts creates a sense of order and peace. This reduction in stress has been linked to improved health, better sleep, and increased overall happiness.

2. **Increased Focus** Clutter competes for your attention, draining your cognitive resources. By clearing your environment and mind, you can concentrate more effectively on the tasks and goals that matter. A minimalist mindset helps you streamline your focus, enabling deeper and more productive work.

3. **Better Decision-Making** Every item you own, every commitment you make, and every thought you entertain demands mental energy. Minimalism reduces decision fatigue by simplifying your choices. This newfound clarity allows you to make decisions more confidently and efficiently, freeing up energy for creativity and problem-solving.

How a Minimalist Mindset Creates Space for Growth and Opportunities

One of the most profound impacts of minimalism is the way it opens up space—physically, mentally, and emotionally—for new growth and opportunities. Here's how:

1. **Physical Space for Clarity** A clutter-free environment fosters a clutter-free mind. By creating an organized and intentional space, you set the stage for creativity, productivity, and peace. When your surroundings support your goals, it becomes easier to focus on them.

2. **Mental Space for Innovation** When your mind is not bogged down by endless to-do lists, unnecessary worries, or irrelevant distractions, you can think more clearly and creatively. This mental clarity often leads to breakthroughs in both personal and professional endeavors.

3. **Emotional Space for Fulfillment** Letting go of toxic relationships, outdated goals, or limiting beliefs creates room for healthier connections, new aspirations, and self-growth. Minimalism empowers you to focus on relationships and activities that nurture your well-being.

4. **Time for What Truly Matters** By streamlining your commitments and prioritizing intentional living, minimalism helps you reclaim your most valuable resource: time. With fewer distractions and obligations, you can devote your energy to the people, projects, and passions that bring you joy.

5. **Opportunities for New Beginnings** When you let go of what no longer serves you, you create space for opportunities that align with your purpose. Whether it's starting a new career, pursuing a passion, or deepening relationships, a minimalist mindset helps you embrace change with open arms.

Conclusion: Laying the Foundation for a Minimalist Life

Minimalism is not an end in itself—it's a tool for building a life that aligns with your deepest values and aspirations. By redefining minimalism as a mindset rather than a lifestyle, you open yourself to its transformative potential. This chapter has laid the foundation for understanding what minimalism truly means and the incredible benefits it offers, especially in today's fast-paced world.

As you continue through this book, you'll discover practical steps to apply minimalism in various areas of your life. Remember, this is your journey, and minimalism will look different for everyone. The key is to start small, focus on what matters most, and allow the minimalist mindset to guide you toward exponential growth and fulfillment.

Chapter 2: Clearing the Mental Clutter

Mental clutter is the invisible barrier that prevents us from thinking clearly, focusing effectively, and living with intention. It often feels like an endless loop of thoughts, worries, and tasks that drain our energy and leave us overwhelmed. To fully embrace the minimalist mindset, it's essential to tackle mental clutter just as you would physical clutter—by identifying its sources, implementing strategies to simplify, and using practical tools to create mental clarity.

This chapter will explore the root causes of mental clutter, provide actionable strategies for clearing your mind, and introduce mindfulness and journaling as transformative tools for mental clarity.

Identifying Sources of Mental Clutter

Mental clutter stems from various internal and external sources. Recognizing these sources is the first step toward reducing the noise in your mind.

1. Overcommitment

- **The Problem:** Agreeing to too many responsibilities—whether at work, in relationships, or personal projects—leads to scattered focus and stress.
- **Why It Happens:** Fear of disappointing others, the desire to please, or the assumption that productivity equals worth can drive overcommitment.
- **Impact on Mental Space:** Overcommitment results in mental exhaustion, reduced efficiency, and a constant feeling of being overwhelmed.

2. Negativity

- **The Problem:** Negative thoughts, self-criticism, and dwelling on past mistakes or future fears clutter your mental space with unproductive patterns.

- **Why It Happens:** Cultural conditioning, personal insecurities, or unresolved trauma can fuel a cycle of negative thinking.
- **Impact on Mental Space:** Negativity consumes mental energy, diminishes confidence, and creates a mental environment of stress and anxiety.

3. Information Overload

- **The Problem:** The modern world bombards us with a constant stream of information—news alerts, emails, social media notifications, and endless content.
- **Why It Happens:** Easy access to information and the pressure to stay "in the know" can lead to overconsumption.
- **Impact on Mental Space:** Excessive information reduces the brain's capacity to process meaningful data, making decision-making and prioritization more difficult.

4. Unfinished Business

- **The Problem:** Tasks, conversations, or unresolved emotional issues that linger in the background of your mind take up valuable mental space.
- **Why It Happens:** Procrastination, avoidance, or a lack of closure can leave loose ends that mentally weigh you down.
- **Impact on Mental Space:** Unfinished business creates a sense of unease and distraction, preventing full engagement with the present.

5. Fear and Worry

- **The Problem:** Fear of failure, fear of the unknown, and persistent worry about things beyond your control create a feedback loop of anxiety.
- **Why It Happens:** A survival mechanism meant to protect us, when unchecked, can spiral into chronic stress.
- **Impact on Mental Space:** Fear and worry occupy cognitive bandwidth, reducing your ability to think clearly or act decisively.

Strategies for Simplifying Thought Processes

Clearing mental clutter requires intentional strategies to streamline your thought processes. By prioritizing what truly matters, you can create space for clarity, focus, and peace.

1. Set Clear Priorities

- **Actionable Steps:**
    - Identify your core values and goals to understand what deserves your focus.
    - Use tools like the Eisenhower Matrix to categorize tasks into urgent, important, and non-essential.
- **Benefit:** Clarity on what matters helps you channel your energy effectively, reducing mental overload.

2. Learn to Say No

- **Actionable Steps:**
    - Practice polite but firm responses when declining unnecessary commitments.
    - Remind yourself that every "yes" to something unimportant is a "no" to your priorities.
- **Benefit:** Saying no protects your time and energy, freeing your mental space for meaningful pursuits.

3. Limit Multitasking

- **Actionable Steps:**
    - Focus on one task at a time to improve efficiency and reduce overwhelm.
    - Use techniques like time blocking to allocate specific periods for tasks.

- **Benefit:** Concentrated effort on a single task reduces mental fragmentation and improves productivity.

4. Curate Your Information Intake

- **Actionable Steps:**
    - Unsubscribe from unnecessary emails and limit social media usage.
    - Designate specific times for consuming news or checking updates.
- **Benefit:** A curated digital environment prevents information overload and allows you to focus on meaningful content.

5. Resolve Unfinished Business

- **Actionable Steps:**
    - Make a list of lingering tasks or unresolved issues and tackle them one at a time.
    - Seek closure through communication or decisive action where possible.
- **Benefit:** Completing unfinished tasks reduces anxiety and creates a sense of accomplishment.

6. Reframe Negative Thoughts

- **Actionable Steps:**
    - Challenge negative beliefs by asking, "Is this thought helpful or true?"
    - Replace unproductive thoughts with constructive affirmations or solutions.
- **Benefit:** Shifting your mindset from negativity to possibility fosters a more positive mental environment.

Tools for Decluttering Your Mind

While strategies provide direction, tools like mindfulness and journaling offer practical ways to consistently clear mental clutter.

1. Mindfulness

- **What It Is:** Mindfulness is the practice of bringing your attention to the present moment without judgment.
- **How to Practice:**
  - Start with short, guided meditations to focus on your breath or bodily sensations.
  - Incorporate mindfulness into daily activities, such as eating or walking, by being fully present.
- **Benefits:** Mindfulness calms the mind, reduces stress, and increases your awareness of mental clutter.

2. Journaling

- **What It Is:** Journaling is the process of writing down your thoughts, emotions, and experiences to gain clarity and perspective.
- **How to Practice:**
  - Use prompts such as "What's taking up space in my mind today?" or "What do I need to let go of?"
  - Engage in freewriting for 10 minutes to unload mental clutter without judgment.
- **Benefits:** Journaling externalizes thoughts, providing relief from mental congestion and helping you identify patterns.

3. Gratitude Practices

- **What It Is:** Focusing on gratitude shifts your mindset from scarcity to abundance.
- **How to Practice:**

- Write down three things you're grateful for each day.
- Reflect on positive moments or achievements before bed.
- **Benefits:** Gratitude reduces negativity and creates a mental environment of positivity and contentment.

Conclusion: Creating Mental Space for Growth

Clearing mental clutter is not a one-time event—it's an ongoing process of intentionality. By identifying the sources of your mental clutter, implementing strategies to simplify your thought processes, and using tools like mindfulness and journaling, you can create the mental clarity necessary for growth and fulfillment.

When you free your mind from unnecessary noise, you open up space for creativity, focus, and peace. This newfound clarity will allow you to approach life's challenges with confidence and seize opportunities with a clear sense of purpose. As you continue your minimalist journey, remember that your mental space is your most valuable asset—treat it with care, and it will reward you with exponential growth and personal transformation.

Chapter 3: Living Small to Think Big

Minimalism is more than a mindset—it's a way of living that influences not only how we think but also how we interact with our physical world. The spaces we inhabit, the tools we use, and the schedules we keep all have a profound effect on our mental clarity, creativity, and ability to innovate. By embracing the principle of "living small," we create an environment that supports big thinking—where ideas, focus, and possibilities can flourish.

In this chapter, we'll explore the connection between your physical surroundings and mental state, offer practical tips for designing a minimalist workspace, home, and schedule, and reveal how minimalism can unlock your creative potential by eliminating distractions.

How Simplifying Your Physical Environment Impacts Your Mental State

Your physical environment is a mirror of your mental state. Cluttered spaces often lead to cluttered minds, while clean, organized surroundings foster a sense of calm and focus. The relationship between your environment and mental well-being is well-documented in psychological research, which shows that the spaces we inhabit can influence stress levels, productivity, and even creativity.

1. Physical Clutter Equals Mental Clutter

- **The Problem:** A messy desk, disorganized room, or overstuffed closet creates visual and cognitive overload, making it harder to focus.
- **The Impact:** Physical clutter sends signals to your brain that your work or life is unfinished, triggering feelings of stress and anxiety.

- **The Solution:** Simplifying your environment reduces these mental triggers, allowing you to think more clearly and feel more at peace.

2. Intentional Spaces Create Intentional Minds

- Minimalist environments encourage intentionality by removing distractions and focusing your attention on what truly matters. When your space reflects your goals and values, it becomes a sanctuary for productive and meaningful work.

3. The Emotional Weight of Stuff

- Excess possessions can carry emotional baggage—guilt from unused items, attachment to outdated belongings, or anxiety about maintaining material things. Letting go of unnecessary items lightens your mental load and fosters emotional freedom.

Tips for Creating a Minimalist Workspace, Home, and Schedule

A minimalist approach to your environment doesn't mean empty walls and sparse furniture—it means curating spaces that support your goals, reduce stress, and spark joy. Here's how to create minimalist spaces that work for you.

1. Designing a Minimalist Workspace

- **Declutter Your Desk:**
  - Keep only essential items within reach: your computer, notebook, pen, and one or two decorative or inspirational objects.
  - Eliminate unnecessary papers by digitizing files and organizing your digital workspace.
- **Streamline Tools:**
  - Invest in multifunctional tools or software to reduce the need for multiple devices or cluttered apps.
- **Personalize with Purpose:**
  - Add a single plant, photo, or piece of art that inspires focus without overwhelming the space.
- **Benefits:** A clean workspace minimizes distractions, improves focus, and signals your brain that it's time to work.

2. Simplifying Your Home

- **Start with One Room:**
  - ◦ Choose a single area to declutter—such as the kitchen, bedroom, or living room—and tackle it systematically.
- **Adopt the "One In, One Out" Rule:**
  - ◦ For every new item you bring into your home, remove an old one to maintain balance.
- **Focus on Functionality:**
  - ◦ Arrange your furniture and belongings to maximize flow and ease of use.
- **Benefits:** A minimalist home fosters relaxation, reduces cleaning time, and creates a sense of order.

3. Creating a Minimalist Schedule

- **Audit Your Commitments:**
  - ◦ List your weekly activities and identify which ones align with your goals and values. Eliminate or delegate the rest.
- **Prioritize Deep Work:**
  - ◦ Allocate blocks of uninterrupted time for tasks that require focus and creativity.
- **Build in Buffer Time:**
  - ◦ Leave unscheduled time in your calendar to account for rest, reflection, and unexpected events.
- **Benefits:** A streamlined schedule reduces stress, increases productivity, and creates space for what truly matters.

How Minimalism Fosters Creativity and Innovative Thinking

One of the greatest advantages of minimalism is its ability to create an environment where creativity and innovation thrive. Here's how living small can inspire big ideas:

1. Fewer Distractions, More Focus

- Clutter—whether physical, digital, or mental—distracts your brain from deep thinking. By removing distractions, you free your cognitive resources to focus fully on creative tasks.

2. Mental Space for New Ideas

- Simplifying your environment creates mental space, allowing your mind to wander, reflect, and connect seemingly unrelated concepts. This state, known as "unstructured thought," is essential for creativity.

3. The Power of Constraints

- Minimalism imposes constraints that can spark innovation. When you limit your tools or resources, you're forced to think more creatively about how to solve problems or achieve your goals.

4. Intentionality Sparks Innovation

- Minimalism encourages intentionality—choosing what to focus on and what to let go of. This clarity helps you identify opportunities, prioritize projects, and innovate effectively.

5. The Role of Calm in Creativity

- A minimalist environment fosters a sense of calm, which is critical for entering a flow state—a highly productive and creative mental state.

Practical Steps to Harness Creativity Through Minimalism
1. Create a "Creative Zone"

- Dedicate a specific area in your home or workspace for creative activities. Keep it free of distractions and filled with only the tools or materials you need.

2. Embrace a "Reset Ritual"

- At the end of each day, take 10 minutes to tidy your workspace, organize your tools, and prepare for the next day. This ritual creates a sense of order and readiness for creative work.

3. Schedule Unstructured Time

- Allow time in your schedule for daydreaming, reflection, or exploration. Some of the best ideas emerge during moments of mental rest.

4. Adopt a "Less is More" Approach

- When brainstorming or problem-solving, focus on simplicity. Ask, "What is the simplest solution?" or "How can I do more with less?"

5. Practice Digital Minimalism

- Limit the number of apps, tabs, or devices you use during creative sessions to maintain focus. Use tools like website blockers if necessary.

Conclusion: Living Small, Thinking Big

Minimalism is not about restricting your life—it's about expanding your mind. By simplifying your physical environment, you create the conditions for clarity, focus, and creativity to flourish. A minimalist workspace, home, and schedule serve as foundations for big thinking, helping you eliminate distractions and prioritize what truly matters.

Living small allows you to think big because it removes the noise and clutter that weigh you down. As you embrace minimalism in your spaces and routines, you'll find that your mind is freer to innovate, dream, and pursue bold ideas. The journey of living small is not about what you give up—it's about what you gain: a life of purpose, clarity, and boundless potential.

Chapter 4: Aligning Goals with Your Minimalist Values

Minimalism isn't just about clearing clutter—it's about clarity in purpose. When your goals align with your values, you create a life that feels both intentional and fulfilling. By focusing on what truly matters and letting go of distractions, you can achieve your aspirations more effectively while maintaining a sense of balance and peace.

This chapter explores how to set clear, minimalist goals rooted in your core values, the transformative power of saying "no" to maximize focus, and techniques for avoiding decision fatigue while staying motivated on your minimalist journey.

Setting Clear, Minimalist Goals That Align with Your Values

The foundation of minimalist goal-setting is intentionality. Instead of pursuing goals because they seem impressive or expected, minimalism encourages you to focus on what aligns with your deepest values and passions. This clarity prevents wasted effort and ensures that every step you take contributes meaningfully to your life.

1. Identify Your Core Values

- **Why It Matters:** Your values act as a compass, guiding your decisions and helping you prioritize goals that resonate with your authentic self.
- **Actionable Steps:**
    - Reflect on moments in your life when you felt the happiest, most fulfilled, or proud. What values were present in those experiences (e.g., creativity, connection, freedom)?
    - Write down your top 5-10 values and keep them visible as a reference when setting goals.

2. Define What Success Means to You

- **Why It Matters:** Society often defines success in terms of money, status, or possessions, but these may not align with your values. Minimalism helps you define success on your own terms.
- **Actionable Steps:**
    - Ask yourself, "What does a meaningful life look like to me?"
    - Align your goals with this vision, focusing on areas like personal growth, relationships, contribution, or well-being.

3. Prioritize Quality Over Quantity

- **Why It Matters:** Pursuing too many goals simultaneously dilutes your focus and energy. A minimalist approach emphasizes depth over breadth.
- **Actionable Steps:**
    - Limit yourself to 3-5 key goals at a time. This ensures you can dedicate the necessary attention and effort to each.
    - Periodically review and adjust your goals to reflect any changes in your priorities or values.

4. Use SMART Goals with a Minimalist Twist

- **Why It Matters:** Specific, measurable, achievable, relevant, and time-bound goals keep you focused and motivated.
- **Minimalist Twist:**
    - Ensure your goals are *relevant* to your values and *specific* enough to avoid unnecessary complexity.
    - Example: Instead of "Get in shape," try "Exercise for 30 minutes, 4 days a week, to improve my energy and well-being."

The Power of Saying "No" to Maximize Focus

Saying "yes" to every opportunity, request, or task may feel like the right thing to do, but it often leads to overcommitment, stress, and diluted focus. Learning to say "no" is a cornerstone of minimalism, allowing you to protect your time and energy for what truly matters.

1. Why Saying "No" Is Empowering

- Saying "no" doesn't mean rejecting people or opportunities—it means affirming your priorities.
- Every "no" to something non-essential is a "yes" to your core values and goals.

2. How to Identify What to Say "No" To

- **Ask Yourself:**
  - Does this align with my goals and values?
  - Will this bring joy, fulfillment, or growth into my life?
  - Is this a true priority, or am I agreeing out of obligation or fear of disappointment?

3. Techniques for Saying "No" Gracefully

- **The Direct Decline:**
  - "I appreciate the offer, but I need to focus on my current commitments."
- **The Delayed Response:**
  - "Let me check my schedule and get back to you." (Use this time to evaluate if the request aligns with your values.)
- **The Conditional Yes:**
  - "I can help with this, but only if we can adjust the timeline or scope."

4. The Impact of Saying "No"

- Saying "no" creates space for deeper focus, reduces stress, and helps you avoid spreading yourself too thin. It also reinforces your boundaries, making it easier to prioritize what truly matters.

Techniques for Avoiding Decision Fatigue and Maintaining Motivation

Minimalism isn't just about eliminating physical clutter—it's also about simplifying decision-making. Every decision you make requires energy, and too many choices can lead to decision fatigue, a state where your ability to make sound judgments diminishes.

1. Streamline Routine Decisions

- **Why It Matters:** Automating or simplifying routine decisions saves mental energy for more important tasks.
- **Actionable Steps:**
    - Adopt a capsule wardrobe with versatile pieces to reduce daily clothing choices.
    - Plan meals or create a weekly menu to eliminate decision-making around food.
    - Use tools like to-do lists or apps to organize tasks in advance.

2. Create a Decision-Making Framework

- **Why It Matters:** A clear framework helps you quickly evaluate options without overthinking.
- **Actionable Steps:**
    - Base decisions on your core values and priorities. For example:
        - Does this align with my current goals?
        - Does this add value to my life, or is it a distraction?
    - If the answer is unclear, consider using a pros and cons list or consulting a trusted friend or mentor.

3. Manage Energy, Not Just Time

- **Why It Matters:** Energy, not time, is often the limiting factor in productivity and motivation.
- **Actionable Steps:**
    - Identify your peak energy times and schedule high-priority tasks during these periods.
    - Take regular breaks to recharge, using techniques like the Pomodoro method or mindfulness exercises.

4. Cultivate Intrinsic Motivation

- **Why It Matters:** Goals aligned with your internal values and passions are more sustainable than those driven by external validation.
- **Actionable Steps:**
    - Reflect on why each goal is meaningful to you. Write down your reasons and revisit them when motivation wanes.
    - Celebrate small milestones to build momentum and maintain enthusiasm.

5. Eliminate Decision Distractions

- **Why It Matters:** Reducing unnecessary choices creates more bandwidth for meaningful decisions.
- **Actionable Steps:**
    - Turn off notifications during focus periods to avoid decision-making about when to engage with distractions.
    - Declutter your workspace and digital environment to remove visual and mental distractions.

Conclusion: Aligning Goals with a Minimalist Life

Aligning your goals with your minimalist values isn't just about simplifying your aspirations—it's about ensuring that every action you take moves you closer to a life of purpose and fulfillment. By setting clear goals rooted in your values, learning to say "no" to distractions, and using techniques to avoid decision fatigue, you can channel your energy and focus toward what truly matters.

Minimalism empowers you to embrace intentionality in every aspect of your life. When your goals reflect your deepest values, and your actions are guided by clarity and purpose, you'll find that the path to success feels not only achievable but deeply rewarding. By living and working in alignment with your minimalist principles, you can think bigger, act smarter, and create a life that truly resonates with your authentic self.

Chapter 5: Growing Big with Minimalism

Minimalism, often misunderstood as a philosophy of limitation, is actually a framework for expansion. By focusing on what truly matters and shedding distractions, the minimalist mindset creates fertile ground for growth—be it in your career, relationships, or personal development. Minimalism doesn't hold you back; it propels you forward by enabling you to invest your energy and resources in meaningful pursuits.

In this chapter, we'll explore how minimalism can drive growth in every area of your life, highlight inspiring success stories of individuals and businesses thriving with minimalism, and provide practical steps to sustain and adapt the minimalist mindset as your life evolves.

How Minimalism Fuels Growth in Key Areas
1. Career Growth

Minimalism empowers you to prioritize high-impact work, streamline decision-making, and focus on long-term goals rather than getting bogged down by distractions.

- **Focus on Impactful Work:**
  - Simplifying your commitments allows you to concentrate on tasks that align with your career aspirations and deliver significant results.
  - Example: A minimalist professional might delegate administrative tasks to focus on strategic planning or skill development.
- **Reduced Decision Fatigue:**
  - By simplifying routines and workflows, you save mental energy for creative and strategic thinking, which are critical for career growth.

- **Networking with Purpose:**
  - Minimalism encourages intentional connections with mentors, colleagues, and peers who align with your professional values and goals.

2. Relationship Growth

Minimalism fosters meaningful relationships by encouraging quality over quantity and helping you invest time and energy in connections that truly matter.

- **Deeper Connections:**
  - Letting go of superficial or toxic relationships creates space for nurturing authentic connections.
  - Example: Instead of attending every social event, a minimalist focuses on meaningful one-on-one interactions with loved ones.
- **Improved Communication:**
  - Minimalism encourages intentionality in conversations, promoting active listening and thoughtful responses.
- **Setting Healthy Boundaries:**
  - By learning to say "no," you protect your time and energy, ensuring that your relationships are balanced and mutually supportive.

3. Personal Development

Minimalism creates an environment where personal growth can thrive by removing distractions and fostering clarity.

- **Clarity of Purpose:**
    - Simplifying your goals and commitments allows you to focus on personal growth areas like education, health, or creativity.
- **Increased Self-Awareness:**
    - Minimalism promotes reflection and mindfulness, helping you identify strengths, weaknesses, and opportunities for self-improvement.
- **Freedom to Explore:**
    - With fewer material and mental burdens, you have more freedom to pursue hobbies, passions, and interests that enrich your life.

Success Stories of Thriving with Minimalism
1. Marie Kondo (Professional Organizer and Author)

- By embracing and teaching the minimalist mindset through her KonMari Method, Kondo built a global brand around the idea of "sparking joy." Her business success illustrates how minimalism can lead to clarity, purpose, and significant professional growth.

2. Steve Jobs (Apple Inc. Co-founder)

- Known for his minimalist approach to design and decision-making, Jobs focused on creating simple, elegant, and functional products. This philosophy of less-is-more drove Apple's growth into one of the world's most valuable companies.

3. Joshua Becker (Founder of Becoming Minimalist)

- Becker transitioned from a life of material accumulation to one of intentional living. By embracing minimalism, he not only transformed his personal life but also inspired millions to simplify their own lives through his books, blog, and speaking engagements.

4. The Tiny House Movement

- Many individuals and families have downsized their living spaces to tiny homes, reducing financial stress and environmental impact while focusing on experiences and relationships. This minimalist lifestyle has led to greater freedom, adventure, and personal fulfillment for countless people.

Practical Steps to Sustain Minimalism and Adapt It as Life Evolves

Minimalism is not a static philosophy—it's a dynamic mindset that evolves with your life. Here are practical steps to ensure that minimalism remains relevant and impactful as your circumstances change.

1. Regularly Reassess Your Values

- **Why:** As you grow and evolve, your priorities and values may shift. Regularly evaluating them ensures that your minimalist lifestyle aligns with your current goals.
- **How:**
    - Set aside time annually to reflect on your core values and whether your lifestyle supports them.
    - Adjust your commitments, possessions, or routines to reflect these changes.

2. Stay Flexible

- **Why:** Life is unpredictable, and rigidity can hinder growth. Flexibility allows you to adapt minimalism to new challenges and opportunities.
- **How:**
    - Embrace the idea that minimalism is a tool, not a set of rules. Use it to navigate transitions like career changes, relationships, or parenthood.

3. Maintain a Decluttering Habit

- **Why:** Clutter—both physical and mental—can creep back into your life over time. Regular decluttering prevents overwhelm.
- **How:**
    - Schedule monthly decluttering sessions to reassess your possessions, commitments, and digital spaces.

  ◦ Ask, "Does this add value to my life?" for each item or task.

4. Focus on Experiences Over Possessions

- **Why:** Experiences often bring more lasting joy and fulfillment than material things.
- **How:**
  - ◦ Invest in travel, learning, or shared moments with loved ones rather than accumulating more belongings.

5. Use Minimalism as a Problem-Solving Tool

- **Why:** Minimalism can help you navigate complex decisions by simplifying options and focusing on what truly matters.
- **How:**
  - ◦ When faced with a challenge, ask yourself, "What's the simplest and most effective solution?"
  - ◦ Eliminate unnecessary steps, distractions, or inputs.

6. Build a Supportive Community

- **Why:** Surrounding yourself with like-minded individuals reinforces your commitment to minimalism and provides encouragement.
- **How:**
  - ◦ Join minimalist communities online or in-person to share experiences, challenges, and inspiration.

Conclusion: Minimalism as a Catalyst for Big Growth

Minimalism isn't about shrinking your life—it's about expanding it in meaningful ways. By simplifying your career, relationships, and personal development, you create space for intentional growth, deeper connections, and greater fulfillment. Success stories from individuals and businesses demonstrate that thriving with minimalism is not only possible but also transformative.

As your life evolves, minimalism will remain a powerful tool for navigating change, fostering creativity, and maintaining focus on what truly matters. By staying aligned with your values, embracing flexibility, and committing to intentional living, you'll discover that living with less truly does empower you to grow big.

Appendix A: 30-Day Minimalist Mindset Challenge

Adopting a minimalist mindset is a transformative journey that begins with small, intentional steps. The 30-Day Minimalist Mindset Challenge provides a practical, step-by-step guide to help you integrate minimalist habits into your daily life. This challenge focuses on decluttering, self-reflection, and goal-setting exercises designed to simplify your environment, clarify your priorities, and foster a mindset of intentional living.

How the Challenge Works

Each day features a specific task that builds on the previous ones, gradually introducing minimalist habits that touch on different aspects of life—physical space, mental clarity, and emotional well-being. These steps are designed to be actionable and adaptable, requiring no more than 30-60 minutes a day.

The 30-Day Challenge: Day-by-Day Breakdown
Week 1: Clearing Physical Clutter

The first week focuses on simplifying your physical environment, which lays the foundation for mental clarity.

- **Day 1: Declutter Your Workspace**
  - Remove everything from your desk and only put back what you use daily.
  - Create a digital folder for work files and delete or archive unnecessary ones.
- **Day 2: Purge Your Closet**
  - Sort clothing into three piles: keep, donate, and discard.
  - Ask yourself: "Does this fit? Have I worn it in the last year? Does it spark joy?"
- **Day 3: Simplify Your Kitchen**
  - Declutter one drawer or cabinet. Discard expired items and donate duplicates.
  - Keep only essential utensils and tools.
- **Day 4: Declutter Your Digital Space**
  - Unsubscribe from unnecessary emails and delete unused apps.
  - Organize your phone and computer files into labeled folders.
- **Day 5: Tackle Sentimental Items**
  - Choose 5 sentimental items and evaluate their significance. Keep only what truly matters.
- **Day 6: Streamline Your Bathroom**
  - Discard expired toiletries and unused products.
  - Organize your essentials into a tidy, accessible system.
- **Day 7: Reflect on Your Week**
  - Journal about how decluttering your physical space has impacted your mental clarity.

- Note areas that still need attention and set intentions for the upcoming week.

Week 2: Cultivating Mental Clarity

This week focuses on clearing mental clutter and fostering habits that promote mindfulness and focus.

- **Day 8: Create a Morning Routine**
  - Design a minimalist morning ritual (e.g., meditation, journaling, or stretching) to start your day with clarity.
- **Day 9: Set Your Priorities**
  - Write down your top 5 priorities in life and compare them to how you currently spend your time.
- **Day 10: Practice Mindful Consumption**
  - Spend the day consuming less information. Limit social media, news, and notifications.
- **Day 11: Declutter Your Mind**
  - Write down everything on your mind (a "brain dump") and sort it into tasks, thoughts, and worries.
  - Address one actionable item from your list.
- **Day 12: Simplify Your Commitments**
  - Review your calendar and commitments. Cancel or delegate at least one non-essential task.
- **Day 13: Introduce Mindfulness Practices**
  - Spend 10 minutes practicing mindfulness meditation or focusing on your breath.
- **Day 14: Reflect on Your Week**
  - Journal about your mental clarity and any shifts in your mindset. Celebrate progress, no matter how small.

Week 3: Aligning with Your Values

This week focuses on connecting your minimalist mindset to your core values and long-term goals.

- **Day 15: Define Your Core Values**
    - Write down 5-10 values that matter most to you. Reflect on how they influence your daily decisions.
- **Day 16: Set Intentional Goals**
    - Choose one personal, one professional, and one relational goal that align with your values.
- **Day 17: Create a Vision Board**
    - Use physical materials or a digital platform to visualize your minimalist-inspired goals and aspirations.
- **Day 18: Simplify Financial Habits**
    - Review your monthly expenses and identify areas to cut back. Set a minimalist budget.
- **Day 19: Focus on Quality Relationships**
    - Spend quality time with a loved one or reach out to someone who adds value to your life.
- **Day 20: Declutter Emotional Baggage**
    - Write a letter (you don't need to send it) to someone you need to forgive or express gratitude to.
- **Day 21: Reflect on Your Week**
    - Journal about how aligning your actions with your values has influenced your mindset and well-being.

Week 4: Sustaining and Expanding Minimalism
In the final week, you'll focus on sustaining minimalist habits and applying them to all areas of your life.

- **Day 22: Build a Capsule Wardrobe**
    - Choose 30-40 versatile clothing items that match your style and needs.
- **Day 23: Plan a Minimalist Day**
    - Dedicate one day to doing only essential tasks and spending time on activities you love.
- **Day 24: Reduce Screen Time**
    - Set limits on your daily screen usage and replace it with an offline activity (reading, walking, etc.).
- **Day 25: Practice Gratitude**
    - Write down 5 things you're grateful for and reflect on how minimalism has enhanced your appreciation for life.
- **Day 26: Embrace "One In, One Out"**
    - Commit to removing one item for every new item you bring into your home moving forward.
- **Day 27: Plan for Long-Term Minimalism**
    - Identify three minimalist habits you'll continue practicing and set reminders to revisit them regularly.
- **Day 28: Create a Minimalist Emergency Kit**
    - Prepare a small kit with essentials for unexpected situations, such as important documents, emergency funds, and necessary supplies.
- **Day 29: Share Your Journey**
    - Talk to friends or share on social media about what you've learned during the challenge to inspire others.

- **Day 30: Reflect and Celebrate**
  - Look back at your progress over the past 30 days. Journal about how minimalism has impacted your mindset and lifestyle.
  - Reward yourself with a minimalist experience, such as a nature walk or quality time with loved ones.

Tips for Success

1. **Start Small:**
   - Focus on one task at a time to avoid overwhelm.
2. **Be Consistent:**
   - Set aside a specific time each day for the challenge.
3. **Celebrate Wins:**
   - Acknowledge progress, no matter how small.
4. **Adapt to Your Needs:**
   - Modify tasks to fit your lifestyle and goals.

Conclusion

The 30-Day Minimalist Mindset Challenge is a practical and empowering way to embrace minimalism in all aspects of life. By gradually adopting minimalist habits, you'll clear physical and mental clutter, align your actions with your values, and lay the foundation for long-term growth and fulfillment. Remember, minimalism is not about perfection but about intentional progress—small, meaningful changes that lead to a life of clarity and purpose.

Appendix B: Minimalism Resources and Tools

Minimalism is a lifelong journey, and having the right resources and tools can make it easier to maintain your minimalist lifestyle and deepen your understanding of the philosophy. This appendix provides curated recommendations for books, apps, podcasts, communities, and worksheets to help you track your progress, stay motivated, and remain intentional as you embrace minimalism.

Recommended Books

Books are a fantastic way to gain insights, practical tips, and inspiration for your minimalist journey. Here are some must-reads:

On Minimalist Philosophy

1. **"The Life-Changing Magic of Tidying Up" by Marie Kondo**
   - A practical and emotional guide to decluttering and organizing your physical space, based on the KonMari Method.
2. **"Essentialism: The Disciplined Pursuit of Less" by Greg McKeown**
   - Focuses on simplifying your life by doing fewer things better and prioritizing what truly matters.
3. **"The Minimalist Home" by Joshua Becker**
   - A room-by-room guide to creating a minimalist home that aligns with your values and goals.

On Mindset and Intentional Living

1. **"Digital Minimalism: Choosing a Focused Life in a Noisy World" by Cal Newport**
   - Explores strategies to declutter your digital life and focus on meaningful digital habits.
2. **"Goodbye, Things: The New Japanese Minimalism" by Fumio Sasaki**
   - An inspiring personal account of how letting go of material possessions leads to freedom and happiness.
3. **"The More of Less: Finding the Life You Want Under Everything You Own" by Joshua Becker**
   - Encourages you to live more purposefully by owning less.

Recommended Apps

Technology can support your minimalist lifestyle by helping you declutter, stay organized, and maintain focus. Here are some minimalist-friendly apps:

Decluttering and Organizing

1. **Tody**
   - Helps you create cleaning schedules to maintain a tidy and minimalist home.
2. **Sortly**
   - A digital inventory app that allows you to track and organize your belongings visually.

Digital Minimalism

1. **Freedom**
   - Blocks distracting websites and apps so you can focus on what matters.
2. **Unroll.Me**
   - Helps you declutter your email inbox by unsubscribing from unnecessary newsletters and spam.

Mindfulness and Focus

1. **Headspace**
   - A meditation app that supports mental clarity and mindfulness practices.
2. **Forest**
   - Encourages you to stay off your phone by growing virtual trees for uninterrupted focus time.

Goal Setting and Tracking

1. **Notion**
   - A flexible workspace app for organizing tasks, goals, and projects in one place.
2. **Habitica**
   - Turns habit-building into a game, motivating you to stay consistent with your minimalist goals.

Recommended Podcasts

Podcasts are an excellent way to stay inspired and learn more about minimalism. Here are some top recommendations:

1. **The Minimalists Podcast**
   - Hosted by Joshua Fields Millburn and Ryan Nicodemus, this podcast explores minimalism's impact on relationships, finances, and personal growth.
2. **Optimal Living Daily**
   - A daily podcast featuring bite-sized reads from the best blogs about minimalism, productivity, and intentional living.
3. **The Ground Up Show**
   - Focuses on simplifying life and pursuing meaningful work, with inspiring interviews from creators and entrepreneurs.
4. **Simplify**
   - Discusses strategies for living a simpler, more focused life in a complex world.
5. **Courage & Clarity**
   - Offers actionable advice for aligning your personal and professional life with minimalist principles.

Recommended Communities

Joining like-minded communities can help you stay accountable, share ideas, and gain inspiration. Here are some great places to connect with other minimalists:

Online Forums and Social Media Groups

1. **Reddit: r/minimalism**
   - A vibrant community for sharing tips, success stories, and challenges in the minimalist journey.
2. **Facebook Groups**
   - Look for groups like "Minimalist Living" or "The Minimalists Community" for support and inspiration.

In-Person Meetups

1. **Meetup.com**
   - Search for minimalist or decluttering meetups in your area to connect with others face-to-face.

Courses and Workshops

1. **The Minimalists' 30-Day Challenge**
   - A guided program by The Minimalists to help you embrace simplicity in all aspects of life.

Worksheets for Tracking Progress and Maintaining Minimalism

To maintain a minimalist lifestyle, it's helpful to use worksheets that keep you organized, reflect on your progress, and set intentions. Below are some ideas for printable or digital worksheets to support your journey.

1. Decluttering Tracker

- **Purpose:** Track the areas of your home or life that you've decluttered and areas still to address.
- **How to Use:** Create a checklist with categories like "Closet," "Kitchen," "Digital Files," etc. Mark off sections as you complete them.

2. Daily Intentions Worksheet

- **Purpose:** Start each day with clarity by setting priorities and intentions.
- **How to Use:** Include sections for your top 3 priorities, one thing to let go of, and an affirmation for the day.

3. Weekly Reflection Journal

- **Purpose:** Reflect on your minimalist progress, successes, and areas for improvement.
- **How to Use:** Use prompts like:
    - What did I simplify this week?
    - What challenges did I face in letting go?

◦ How has minimalism improved my life this week?

4. Values Alignment Chart

- **Purpose:** Ensure your goals and actions align with your core values.
- **How to Use:** List your top values and evaluate whether your weekly activities support them. Adjust as needed.

5. Minimalist Budget Tracker

- **Purpose:** Simplify your finances and reduce unnecessary spending.
- **How to Use:** Track income, expenses, and savings goals while identifying non-essential purchases to eliminate.

6. Capsule Wardrobe Planner

- **Purpose:** Curate a versatile wardrobe with fewer, high-quality items.
- **How to Use:** List essential clothing items by category (tops, bottoms, outerwear, shoes) and build your wardrobe around them.

Conclusion

Minimalism is a deeply personal and evolving journey, but having the right resources and tools can make it more accessible and sustainable. From insightful books and practical apps to inspiring podcasts and supportive communities, the options in this appendix are designed to help you stay motivated and intentional as you embrace a minimalist lifestyle.

The included worksheets offer a structured way to track your progress, reflect on your growth, and maintain alignment with your values. Whether you're just starting or looking to deepen your practice, these resources will serve as invaluable companions on your path to simplicity, clarity, and fulfillment.

<u>Message from the Author:</u>

I hope you enjoyed this book, I love astrology and knew there was not a book such as this out on the shelf. I love metaphysical items as well. Please check out my other books:

-Life of Government Benefits

-My life of Hell

-My life with Hydrocephalus

-Red Sky

-World Domination:Woman's rule

-World Domination:Woman's Rule 2: The War

-Life and Banishment of Apophis: book 1

-The Kidney Friendly Diet

-The Ultimate Hemp Cookbook

-Creating a Dispensary(legally)

-Cleanliness throughout life: the importance of showering from childhood to adulthood.

-Strong Roots: The Risks of Overcoddling children

-Hemp Horoscopes: Cosmic Insights and Earthly Healing

- Celestial Hemp Navigating the Zodiac: Through the Green Cosmos

-Astrological Hemp: Aligning The Stars with Earth's Ancient Herb

-The Astrological Guide to Hemp: Stars, Signs, and Sacred Leaves

-Green Growth: Innovative Marketing Strategies for your Hemp Products and Dispensary

-Cosmic Cannabis

-Astrological Munchies

-Henry The Hemp

-Zodiacal Roots: The Astrological Soul Of Hemp

- **Green Constellations: Intersection of Hemp and Zodiac**

-Hemp in The Houses: An astrological Adventure Through The Cannabis Galaxy

-Galactic Ganja Guide

Heavenly Hemp

Zodiac Leaves

Doctor Who Astrology

Cannastrology

Stellar Satvias and Cosmic Indicas

Celestial Cannabis: A Zodiac Journey

AstroHerbology: The Sky and The Soil: Volume 1

AstroHerbology:Celestial Cannabis:Volume 2

Cosmic Cannabis Cultivation

The Starry Guide to Herbal Harmony: Volume 1

The Starry Guide to Herbal Harmony: Cannabis Universe: Volume 2

Yugioh Astrology: Astrological Guide to Deck, Duels and more

Nightmare Mansion: Echoes of The Abyss

Nightmare Mansion 2: Legacy of Shadows

Nightmare Mansion 3: Shadows of the Forgotten

Nightmare Mansion 4: Echoes of the Damned

The Life and Banishment of Apophis: Book 2

Nightmare Mansion: Halls of Despair

Healing with Herb: Cannabis and Hydrocephalus

Planetary Pot: Aligning with Astrological Herbs: Volume 1

Fast Track to Freedom: 30 Days to Financial Independence Using AI, Assets, and Agile Hustles

Cosmic Hemp Pathways

How to Become Financially Free in 30 Days: 10,000 Paths to Prosperity

Zodiacal Herbage: Astrological Insights: Volume 1

Nightmare Mansion: Whispers in the Walls

The Daleks Invade Atlantis

Henry the hemp and Hydrocephalus

10X The Kidney Friendly Diet

Cannabis Universe: Adult coloring book

Hemp Astrology: The Healing Power of the Stars

Zodiacal Herbage: Astrological Insights: Cannabis Universe: Volume 2

<u>Planetary Pot: Aligning with Astrological Herbs: Cannabis Universes: Volume 2</u>

Doctor Who Meets the Replicators and SG-1: The Ultimate Battle for Survival

Nightmare Mansion: Curse of the Blood Moon

<u>The Celestial Stoner: A Guide to the Zodiac</u>

Cosmic Pleasures: Sex Toy Astrology for Every Sign

Hydrocephalus Astrology: Navigating the Stars and Healing Waters

Lapis and the Mischievous Chocolate Bar

Celestial Positions: Sexual Astrology for Every Sign

Apophis's Shadow Work Journal: : A Journey of Self-Discovery and Healing

Kinky Cosmos: Sexual Kink Astrology for Every Sign

Digital Cosmos: The Astrological Digimon Compendium

Stellar Seeds: The Cosmic Guide to Growing with Astrology

Apophis's Daily Gratitude Journal

Cat Astrology: Feline Mysteries of the Cosmos

The Cosmic Kama Sutra: An Astrological Guide to Sexual Positions

Unleash Your Potential: A Guided Journal Powered by AI Insights

Whispers of the Enchanted Grove

Cosmic Pleasures: An Astrological Guide to Sexual Kinks

369, 12 Manifestation Journal

Whisper of the nocturne journal(blank journal for writing or drawing)

The Boogey Book

Locked In Reflection: A Chastity Journey Through Locktober

Generating Wealth Quickly:

How to Generate $100,000 in 24 Hours

Star Magic: Harness the Power of the Universe

The Flatulence Chronicles: A Fart Journal for Self-Discovery

The Doctor and The Death Moth

Seize the Day: A Personal Seizure Tracking Journal

The Ultimate Boogeyman Safari: A Journey into the Boogie World and Beyond

Whispers of Samhain: 1,000 Spells of Love, Luck, and Lunar Magic: Samhain Spell Book

Apophis's guides:

Witch's Spellbook Crafting Guide for Halloween

<u>Frost & Flame: The Enchanted Yule Grimoire of 1000 Winter Spells</u>

<u>The Ultimate Boogey Goo Guide & Spooky Activities for Halloween Fun</u>

Harmony of the Scales: A Libra's Spellcraft for Balance and Beauty

The Enchanted Advent: 36 Days of Christmas Wonders

Nightmare Mansion: The Labyrinth of Screams

Harvest of Enchantment: 1,000 Spells of Gratitude, Love, and Fortune for Thanksgiving

The Boogey Chronicles: A Journal of Nightly Encounters and Shadowy Secrets

The 12 Days of Financial Freedom: A Step-by-Step Christmas Countdown to Transform Your Finances

Sigil of the Eternal Spiral Blank Journal

A Christmas Feast: Timeless Recipes for Every Meal

Cosmic Sales: The Astrological Guide to Black Friday Shopping

Legends of the Corn Mother and Other Harvest Myths

Whispers of the Harvest: The Corn Mother's Journal

The Evergreen Spellbook

The Doctor Meets the Boogeyman

The White Witch of Rose Hall's SpellBook

The Gingerbread Golem's Shadow: A Study in Sweet Darkness

The Gingerbread Golem Codex: An Academic Exploration of Sweet Myths

The Gingerbread Golem Grimoire: Sweet Magicks and Spells for the Festive Witch

The Curse of the Gingerbread Golem

10-minute Christmas Crafts for kids

<u>Christmas Crisis Solutions: The Ultimate Last-Minute Survival Guide</u>

Gingerbread Golem Recipes: Holiday Treats with a Magical Twist

The Infinite Key: Unlocking Mystical Secrets of the Ages

Enchanted Yule: A Wiccan and Pagan Guide to a Magical and Memorable Season

Dinosaurs of Power: Unlocking Ancient Magick

Astro-Dinos: The Cosmic Guide to Prehistoric Wisdom

Gallifrey's Yule Logs: A Festive Doctor Who Cookbook

The Dino Grimoire: Secrets of Prehistoric Magick

The Gift They Never Knew They Needed

The Gingerbread Golem's Culinary Alchemy: Enchanting Recipes for a Sweetly Dark Feast

A Time Lord Christmas: Holiday Adventures with the Doctor

Krampusproofing Your Home: Defensive Strategies for Yule

Silent Frights: A Collection of Christmas Creepypastas to Chill Your Bones

Santa Raptor's Jolly Carnage: A Dino-Claus Christmas Tale

Prehistoric Palettes: A Dino Wicca Coloring Journey

The Christmas Wishkeeper Chronicles

The Starlight Sleigh: A Holiday Journey

Elf Secrets: The True Magic of the North Pole

Candy Cane Conjurations

Cooking with Kids: Recipes Under 20 Minutes

Doctor Who: The TARDIS Confiscation

The Anxiety First Aid Kit: Quick Tools to Calm Your Mind

Frosty Whispers: A Winter's Tale

The Infinite Key: Unlocking the Secrets to Prosperity, Resilience, and Purpose

The Grasping Void: Why You'll Regret This Purchase

Astrology for Busy Bees: Star Signs Simplified

The Instant Focus Formula: Cut Through the Noise

The Secret Language of Colors: Unlocking the Emotional Codes

Sacred Fossil Chronicles: Blank Journal

The Christmas Cottage Miracle

Feeding Frenzy: Graboid-Inspired Recipes

Manifest in Minutes: The Quick Law of Attraction Guide

The Symbiote Chronicles: Doctor Who's Venomous Journey

If you want solar for your home go here: https://www.harborso-lar.live/apophisenterprises/

Get Some Tarot cards: https://www.makeplayingcards.com/sell/apophis-occult-shop

Get some shirts: https://www.bonfire.com/store/apophis-shirt-emporium/

<u>Instagrams:</u>
@apophis_enterprises,
@apophisbookemporium,
@apophisscardshop
Twitter: @apophisenterpr1
Tiktok:@apophisenterprise
Youtube: @sg1fan23477, @FiresideRetreatKingdom
Hive: @sg1fan23477
CheeLee: @SG1fan23477

Podcast: Apophis Chat Zone: https://open.spotify.com/show/5zXbrCLEV2xzCp8ybrfHsk?si=fb4d4fdbdce44dec

Newsletter: https://apophiss-newsletter-27c897.beehiiv.com/

If you want to support me or see posts of other projects that I have come over to: **buymeacoffee.com/mpetchinskg**
I post there daily several times a day

Get your Dinowicca or Christmas themed digital products, especially Santa Raptor songs and other musics. Here: **https://sg1fan23477.gumroad.com**

Apophis Yuletide Digital has not only digital Christmas items, but it will have all things with Dinowicca as well as other Digital products.

www.ingramcontent.com/pod-product-compliance
Lightning Source LLC
Chambersburg PA
CBHW070555160726
48003CB00005B/2058